CUB REPORTER

MEETS FAMOUS AMERICANS

WHAT'S YOUR STORY, SUSAN B. ANTHONY?

Krystyna Poray Goddu
illustrations by Doug Jones

Lerner Publications ◆ Minneapolis

Note to readers, parents, and educators:
This book includes an interview of a famous American. While the words this person speaks are not her actual words, all the information in the book is true and has been carefully researched.

Text and illustrations copyright © 2016 by Lerner Publishing Group, Inc.

All rights reserved. International copyright secured. No part of this book may be reproduced, stored in a retrieval system, or transmitted in any form or by any means—electronic, mechanical, photocopying, recording, or otherwise—without the prior written permission of Lerner Publishing Group, Inc., except for the inclusion of brief quotations in an acknowledged review.

Lerner Publications Company
A division of Lerner Publishing Group, Inc.
241 First Avenue North
Minneapolis, MN 55401 USA

For reading levels and more information, look up this title at www.lernerbooks.com.

Main body text set in Avenir LT Pro 45 Book 15/21. Typeface provided by Linotype AG.

Library of Congress Cataloging-in-Publication Data

Goddu, Krystyna Poray.
    What's your story, Susan B. Anthony? / Krystyna Poray Goddu.
        pages cm — (Cub reporter meets famous Americans)
    Includes bibliographical references and index.
    ISBN 978-1-4677-8785-7 (lb : alk. paper) — ISBN 978-1-4677-9649-1 (pb : alk. paper) — ISBN 978-1-4677-9650-7 (eb pdf)
    1. Anthony, Susan B. (Susan Brownell), 1820–1906—Juvenile literature.
2. Feminists—United States—Biography—Juvenile literature. 3. Suffragists—United States—Biography—Juvenile literature. 4. Women's rights—United States—History—Juvenile literature. 5. Women—Suffrage—United States—History—Juvenile literature. I. Title.
HQ1413.A55G63 2016
305.42092—dc23 [B]   2015018659

Manufactured in the United States of America
1 – VP – 12/31/15

Table of Contents

Hi, everyone! Today I'm talking to a very important person from American history. Her name is Susan B. Anthony. Susan, would you tell us why you're important?

Susan says: I'd be happy to. I fought for equal rights for women. When I was a girl, women didn't have the same rights they have today. Men were in charge of households and usually had the final say on all decisions. Many women weren't allowed to go to school or to work outside their homes. Married women couldn't own property or have their own money. And women couldn't vote. That seemed very unfair to me. So I worked to change those things.

Susan B. Anthony as a young woman

When and where were you born?

Susan says: I was born on February 15, 1820, in Adams, Massachusetts. I was the second of six children. My father was a **Quaker**. This religious group believes that all people are equal. Quakers are against violence and war. They believe in living plain and simple lives. My brothers, sisters, and I couldn't dance or listen to music. We couldn't play with toys. We couldn't even wear bright colors.

Susan's parents lived simple lives and raised Susan to do the same.

How did your family spend their time?

Susan says: I played a lot of make-believe with my brothers and sisters. But we also had chores. My father built a mill where young women worked to make cotton. They came from other towns and lived with our family. My mother cooked and cleaned for them and washed their clothes. It was a lot of work. We children had to help. I also liked to read and write. I learned to read around the age of four. Many people didn't believe girls should go to school, but my father did. He even built a school onto our home for the neighborhood children. I went to school there myself for a number of years.

Susan's father built a mill like this one in Massachusetts.

What did you do when you finished school?

Susan says: I took a job at a Quaker school for girls in New Rochelle, New York. I taught at different schools for ten years, until I was twenty-nine. But in New Rochelle, I saw something that set me down a different path. At a Quaker meeting, I saw some white people walk out because a black man was there. I was shocked. All the Quakers I knew believed black people and white people were equals. But many white people at that time thought they were better than African Americans. Those who walked out of the meeting were among them. My father encouraged me to start speaking out for fairness for everyone, from black people to women and children.

Susan supervised students' lessons for ten years as a teacher in classrooms like this one.

Did you start to make speeches then?

Susan says: I did. But the first speeches I made didn't have to do with race. They had to do with another fairness issue I cared deeply about. The issue was how alcohol affected women.

Some women had husbands who drank too much. Sometimes women's husbands hurt them after drinking too much. And some husbands spent all their families' money on alcohol. Women couldn't do anything about these problems. So I began speaking out to **ban** alcohol. In 1852, I went to an anti-alcohol **convention** in New York. There I saw something else that made me want to keep fighting for fairness.

This picture from 1874 shows women destroying barrels of alcohol. Susan didn't really do this, but she did feel strongly that alcohol use could harm families.

Susan says: I saw that women didn't have the same right to speak as men. When I tried to speak, I was told that women had been invited only to listen. I was so mad that I walked out. Some other women followed me.

Around that time, I met a woman named Elizabeth Cady Stanton. She supported women's rights too. She had even written a **declaration** saying women should be treated as men's equals in every way. My experience in New York made me want to join Elizabeth to fight for women's rights. She liked this idea. We decided we would work together for women's **equality**.

Elizabeth Cady Stanton fought for women's rights.

What did you do to gain more rights for women?

Susan says: Elizabeth wrote speeches about why women should have equal rights. Then I traveled around the country giving those speeches. Elizabeth was a good writer. She could speak well too, but she was married and had children. Women who had families were not free to travel. I wasn't married, so I could travel more easily.

I often went to Elizabeth's home in Seneca Falls, New York, and we planned what the speeches would be about. I provided facts to help Elizabeth write the speeches. And many times, I looked after her children while she wrote.

Susan *(second from left, front)* and Elizabeth *(fourth from left, front)* worked hard to spread the message of equality.

What results came about because of your work?

Susan says: A change that made me very proud happened in 1860. A law was passed in New York that allowed some women to have a say in what happened to their children, their property, and any money they earned. That was a big step. But other changes were slow in coming. It was hard to keep people interested in women's rights. Most people were more concerned with **slavery**. Slavery was common then. Many white people in the South owned black slaves. Elizabeth and I were concerned with slavery too. So we worked to get a law passed that banned slavery. The law passed! Then we turned back to women's rights.

Slaves were forced to work without pay.

What steps did you take next?

Susan says: We started a group that worked to get women the right to vote. We believed that women should have an equal say in what happened in the United States and in their own states and cities. We also started a newspaper called the *Revolution*. In it, we published information and ideas about why women should have the right to vote. When black men got the right to vote in 1869, I thought that women would get the same right very soon. I was wrong. So when it was time for the presidential election in 1872, I decided I had to take a big stand.

The Revolution.

PRINCIPLE, NOT POLICY: JUSTICE, NOT FAVORS.—MEN, THEIR RIGHTS AND NOTHING MORE: WOMEN, THEIR RIGHTS AND NOTHING LESS.

VOL. I.—NO. 2.   NEW YORK, WEDNESDAY, JANUARY 15, 1868. $2.00 A YEAR.

TEXAS RECONSTRUCTION.

Scarcely a week passes in which there are not frequent murders in Texas of Union men, officers as well as others, white as well as black, and generally they go unavenged, the murderers even boasting of their bloody work! The San Antonio *Express* states that on Friday, Nov. 15, Capt. C. E. Culver, the Bureau Agent stationed at Cotton Gin, Freestone County, and his orderly, were murdered three miles north of Springfield, Limestone County. It appears that Capt. Culver had some little difficulty with one Wm. Stewart, and this same Stewart claims to have killed both Capt. Culver and his orderly, and says they fired on him first; but, strange to say, they were shot with different guns. Capt. Culver's head was also cut asunder—done with an axe or some other sharp instrument. There was a large bullet-hole through his right breast, and there was no hole in the shirts or vest Capt. Culver had on at the time he was killed. It is strange that a large ball should pass through a man's body and not through the clothes he had on at the time. It is a great mystery. Capt. Culver was an active member of the Union League of America, and was to open a Council

path—amending the Constitution—but thus far without success. The vote in 1846 was 85,406 for, and 224,336 against impartial suffrage; in 1860 there were 197,503 in favor, and 337,984 opposed.

"The question is naturally up again in the present Convention, and may in due time come before the people; but past experience gives little hope for the friends of impartial suffrage. In the votes noted above, the Democratic party conspicuously opposed the repeal of the property qualification; a few, doubtless, voted the right way, but where one Democrat voted 'Yes,' probably ten Republicans voted 'No.'"

HOME TRUTHS.

Eliza Archard, in the *Herald of Health* has a long article, full of wholesome Rye and Indian truths, like these below—good for kitchen or parlor.

If one should say: "Muscle and Manhood," it would be nothing either strange or unusual, merely an alliteration for the well recognized fact that man is an animal. For muscle and manhood run together by nature. But who

gentleman was a man of average muscle; the four girls, as ladies go, had decidedly more than the average of physical strength.

And this is what four full-grown girls amount to! But something very like the millennium will approach before women can be made to understand that they ought to be ashamed to let one man have more strength than four women. This is the worst of it all. It is their *religious conviction* that the crowning glory of womankind is physical degeneracy. Their chief delight is to believe themselves born to cling to whatever is nearest, in a droopy, like the ivy-to-the-oak way, and to be viney, and twiney, and whiney throughout. Like the ivy to the oak, exactly, if we are willing to learn anything from nature; for, in point of fact, the ivy generally smothers the oak to death at last.

"Woman conquers by her weakness." Woman's weakness, indeed! Woman's nonsense! Woman's weakness is despicable. Weakness of any kind is a credit to nobody. How can it be? Do we admire a man more because one arm is paralyzed, or because he is blind of an eye? Is there anything particularly lovely in the ghastly sight of a man who is starving to death? And what more claim to our admiration has a

How did you take a stand in 1872?

Susan says: My three sisters and I went to the **polling place** where the men were voting for president. We demanded to vote. At first, the men in charge wouldn't let us. But I read them the law that allowed black men to vote. It said all citizens have the right to vote. Women are citizens, I said, and so we have the right to vote. Finally, they let us vote. It was so exciting! But two weeks later, I was arrested for voting.

In 1888, women were allowed to vote in some local elections. Here women wait in line to cast their ballots.

What happened after you were arrested?

Susan says: I had to go to court. There, a judge would decide if I was **guilty** or not. The judge wouldn't let me speak while I was in court. And he said he had to find me guilty. My punishment was to pay a fine. I refused to pay it. I thought then that the judge would send me to jail. But he didn't. He decided that he didn't want me to get any more attention for demanding women's voting rights.

Susan never backed down in her fight for voting rights.

What did you do after going to court?

Susan says: I continued to travel and make speeches. And it paid off! Women eventually won the right to vote in Wyoming, Colorado, Utah, and Idaho. But I wanted women everywhere in the country to gain the right to vote. So I kept speaking.

Elizabeth and I also wrote a book about the quest for women's rights. We ended up publishing three big volumes. I preferred speaking to writing, though. I went from state to state, telling people to keep on fighting. I told them that failure was impossible.

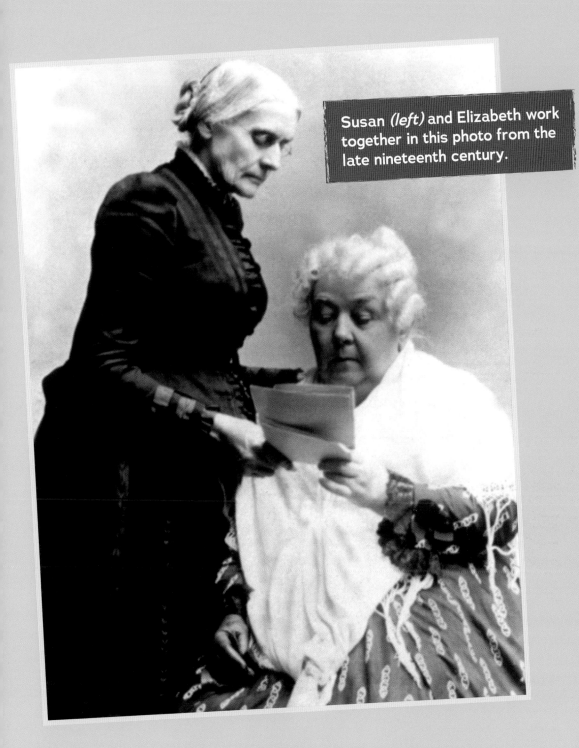

Susan *(left)* and Elizabeth work together in this photo from the late nineteenth century.

How did your life and work make a difference?

Susan says: My work changed many people's minds about women's equality. Together, Elizabeth and I helped win rights for women that they'd never had before. Women throughout the country finally got the right to vote in 1920. I'm proud to say that I helped make that happen.

Timeline

1820   Susan B. Anthony is born in Adams, Massachusetts.

1839   Susan starts her first teaching job.

1849   Susan begins speaking out against drinking alcohol. Soon after this, she meets Elizabeth Cady Stanton and joins the fight for women's rights.

1860   New York State passes a law giving some women more control over their families and property.

1868   Susan and Elizabeth begin publishing the *Revolution.*

1872   Susan votes in the presidential election.

1873   Susan goes to trial and is found guilty of voting.

1881   Susan and Elizabeth publish volume one of the *History of Woman Suffrage*, a book about the quest for women's voting rights.

1902   Elizabeth dies.

1906   Susan dies.

1920   The Nineteenth Amendment to the Constitution gives women the right to vote.

Glossary

ban: to forbid

convention: a large meeting of people who come to the same place to discuss shared interests

declaration: an official statement

equality: the state of having the same rights

guilty: responsible for doing something wrong or something that is against the law

polling place: a place where people go to vote in an election

Quaker: a member of a religious group whose members dress simply, are against violence, and believe all people are equal

slavery: the practice of one person owning another and forcing him or her to work without pay

Further Information

Books

Murphy, Claire Rudolf. *Marching with Aunt Susan: Susan B. Anthony and the Fight for Women's Suffrage.* Atlanta: Peachtree, 2011. This picture book follows a ten-year-old girl in California who meets Susan B. Anthony and helps in the fight for women's rights.

Pollack, Pam, Meg Belviso, and Mike Lacey. *Who Was Susan B. Anthony?* New York: Grosset & Dunlap, 2014. Check out this chapter book biography to learn more details about Susan B. Anthony's life.

Shaffer, Jody Jensen. *What's Your Story, Frederick Douglass?* Minneapolis: Lerner Publications, 2016. Come along as Cub Reporter interviews antislavery activist Frederick Douglass, who was a close friend of Susan B. Anthony.

Websites

Ducksters: Susan B. Anthony
http://www.ducksters.com/biography/susan_b_anthony.php
This site includes a biography about Susan B. Anthony as well as links to other biographies of civil rights heroes and women leaders.

National Susan B. Anthony Museum & House
http://susanbanthonyhouse.org/index.php
Visit this site to see photos of the house Susan B. Anthony lived in from 1866 until her death in 1906.

Index

Photo Acknowledgments

The images in this book are used with the permission of: © GraphicaArtis/Getty Images, p. 5; Courtesy of the Department of Rare Books, Special Collections and Preservation, University of Rochester River Campus Libraries, p. 7 (all); © North Wind Picture Archives/Alamy, p. 9; © Basile De Loose/Fine Art Photographic/Getty Images, p. 11; © CORBIS, pp. 13, 17, 25; © Pictorial Press Ltd/Alamy, p. 15; © Louie Psyihoyos/CORBIS, p. 19; Courtesy Wikimedia Commons, p. 21; © FPG/Getty Images, p. 23; © Everett Collection Historical/Alamy, p. 27.

Front cover: © PhotoQuest/Archive Photos/Getty Images.